Youtube Marketing for Realtors
By Marc Bullard

Marc Bullard
bullard.marc@gmail.com
MarcBullard.com

Video marketing has grown exponentially as a reliable and cheap (yes, cheap) method to market every product under the sun. The interesting thing I have noticed is that many real estate agents rarely use this powerful tool to market not only individual homes but also their business as a whole. Why this is, I can only guess, but I do know that this means agents that are using video are leaps and bounds ahead of their competition.
According to Inman.com, 85% of buyers and sellers want to work with an agent who uses video. Additionally, homes listed with video get four times the inquiries of homes listed without video. So what are you waiting for?

I know what you're waiting for: somebody to show you how to do it. That's where this handy guide comes in, it will show you exactly what to do and just as importantly what not to do. So let's get started.

There are many video sharing sites around on the Internet but the main site you need to be using is Youtube. Most people are familiar with Youtube yet many aren't aware of the power Youtube contains. With 51% audience share Youtube is now the top video research destination for house hunters - even more popular than listing websites! That's not all, Youtube is now the second largest search engine in the world, right behind Google. That's right, people are searching on Youtube just like they would on Google, Bing, etc. And speaking of Google, they own Youtube and repeatedly look at Youtube search results to gather its own results. Plus, Youtube videos appear in Google's results.

Two Youtube videos appear in the top of Google's results.

Think about this, how many results come up in Google when somebody searches "homes for sale virginia beach". Over 9 million.

If you type the same results in Youtube you get a different number, around 300,000 results.

What do you think would be easier to get on the first page of the results? Answer, Youtube. And, if you rank on the first page of results on Youtube there is a better chance of your video appearing on Google's first page as well. It's a double whammy! I have even more good news. You can achieve first page results **for free**. These are not ads, you are not paying to get first page results. All you need to do is post videos and let them work for you.

That covers **why** you need to start using Youtube but it doesn't cover **how**. And how you use Youtube is important. I want you to work smarter, not harder so I've listed exactly what you need to do in order to dominate real estate on Youtube (and possibly Google).

1. The first thing you need is a Youtube account. Youtube accounts are free and available to anybody that has a Gmail account (also free). Most reputable realtors have a Gmail account so therefor have a Youtube account associated with that. You want to be sure you have a Gmail account specifically for your business. Don't use a personal Gmail account. There's no difference between a personal and business

account - and you can have multiple Gmail accounts - so determine what one you want to use for business and only use it for that.

2. Once you have a Youtube account go to youtube.com and log in. You'll know if you're logged in because in the upper right corner a small circle will appear. If you don't see a circle, you will see a button to 'Sign in'. Once signed in, you need to go to your own channel. Click the small circle in the upper right and choose 'My Channel'.

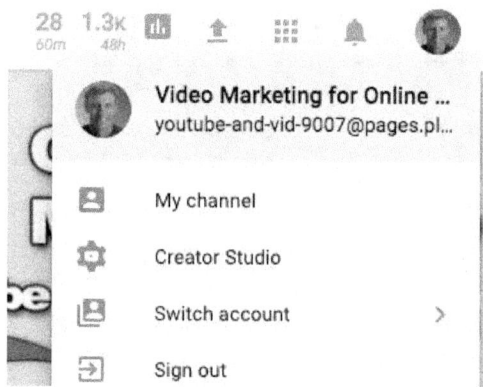

What is a Youtube channel? It is a page on Youtube specifically for you and your videos. Other users can visit your channel page and see your videos as well as other important information for your business. Channels are valuable because there aren't other user's videos on this page. This helps keep your visitors from clicking away to other people's videos. When you get to your channel you will see a large rectangular banner at the top.

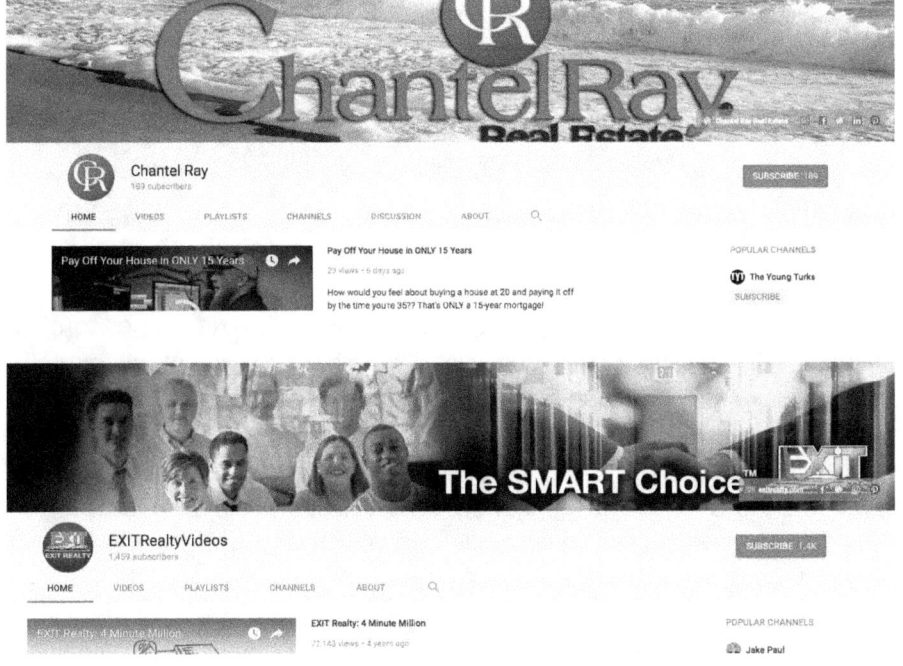

Examples of Real Estate Channel Banners.

The above examples of channel banners show an image as well as some text incorporated in the image. The Chantel Ray banner lets visitors know the name of the company and that it is a real estate company, however the graphic is cut off and very little information is visible. The example below that is for Exit Realty. The image is not home related and the text 'The SMART Choice' is vague at best; it doesn't let visitors know what this channel is about.

Although both banners above are a good start, they could be better. You should use your banner to let visitors know exactly what this channel is about. Use this space to provide as much information as possible (without overcrowding).

The above example is for San Diego Home Company. The banner contains text letting the visitor know exactly what their channel is about (although the font options are questionable) as well as a number to contact. This is better.

Why was the Chantel Ray banner cut off? Well, it's a little technical but basically Youtube gives you the option to upload whatever graphic you want. Youtube is also trying to accommodate screens for smart TVs, tablets, phones, and desktops, all of which have different screen sizes. Youtube provides a template to create your banner image. In the template, it shows precisely what each device will show. Whoever created the graphic didn't fit all of the text in the template area for desktops, causing some to be cut off. This is easily fixed by editing the image and making the text slightly smaller to all be visible in the desktop area.

3. Under the banner you may or may not see available tabs, such as: HOME, VIDEOS, PLAYLISTS, CHANNELS, DISCUSSION, and ABOUT. The San Diego Home Company example above contains these tabs. You want these tabs to be visible on your channel.

This channel is set to the default layout. There are no tabs and no banner.

You need to turn on the option to show tabs. To do this, click the small gear icon located under your banner.

Gear Icon.

Once the gear icon is clicked, a box will appear with an option to customize the layout of your channel. Turn this option on and click save.

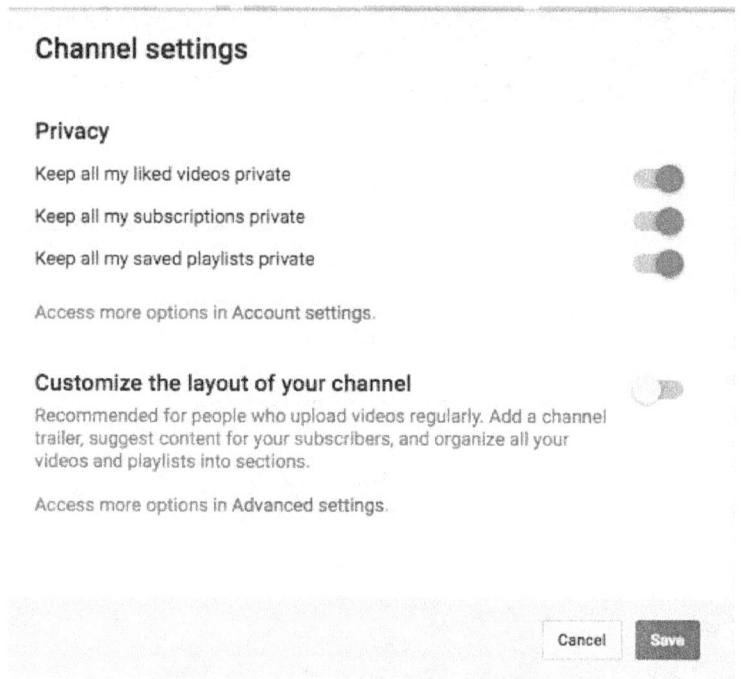

The grey button turns on customization.

Once customization is turned on for your channel, the tabs will appear, including a very important tab: ABOUT.

    4. The ABOUT tab is used to describe your channel as well as provide a business email and links to other websites. This channel description is extremely valuable because any and all information in the channel description is searchable by Youtube and Google. I highly recommend you fill up the description with information about your business, paying particular attention to words and phrases that customers will be typing into the search engines. I'm not a real estate expert, but I am a Youtube expert. I won't know every word or phrase a potential customer will be using. But, I have provided a list to get you started.

Residential, Commercial, Land, Lots, Business Opportunities, Rentals, Property Management, Relocation, Luxury Homes, Sell a house, Buy a house, Homes for sale, Realty, Real estate, Moving, etc.

The above phrases are known as 'keywords'. Keywords are terms that are potentially typed into the search results that are related to real estate. I say 'potentially' because determining keywords is a guessing game, although an educated one. You as the professional might know other keywords your customers could use. Feel free to add those into your description as well.

Important Notes:
A. DO NOT simply add keywords into your description as a list. You want to include them in sentences and paragraphs in a natural way.
B. DO NOT put URLs in your description. They are not click-able and take up important space in your description. You only are allowed up to 2000 characters in your description.
C. Another thing to remember about almost every aspect of Youtube is that nothing is ever set in stone. You can make changes continually in order to maximize your channel and get it exactly how you want.

5. Below the channel description is an area for a business email. I highly recommend adding an email in this area. Under the business email area is a section for you to provide links. This is another very important area. Links provide your visitors with other means to connect with you and there aren't many other areas in all of Youtube that let you add a click-able link. Youtube doesn't want viewers leaving Youtube (imagine that) so they only allow external links in a few places; the ABOUT page is one of these places.

Description

Explore the world's most extraordinary luxury homes and properties for sale. Experience international lifestyles including waterfront, golf or ski luxury homes, properties and estates.

The Sotheby's International Realty® is a global luxury real estate company with a brand's that goes back to 1744, when the venerable Sotheby's Auction House was established. The brand was founded in 1976 to service the real estate needs of the most prestigious clientele in the world.

Links

sothebysrealty.com   Facebook

Twitter   Instagram

LinkedIn   Pintrest

Google+

Sotheby's ABOUT page.

The above example is for Sotheby's Youtube page. Although the description could be better, they did a good job with their Links. The first link is for their main website, and it should be. The first link is extra special and I'll show you why in a second. The other links are for social media sites. This is a good idea as well. If they had other websites I would suggest adding them in there too. All of these links are click-able and once they are added to the Links area, they are visible somewhere else.

Sotheby's channel banner.

The above is a closeup of Sotheby's channel banner. Overlaid on their banner is a series of click-able links. The first one is their website followed by multiple social media links. These are all overlaid on the channel once you add them to the Links area which was over on the ABOUT page. See why the first link is the most important? It appears as the full, readable link.

How do you add links to the ABOUT page? Make sure you're logged in and on the ABOUT page. Hover your mouse over the Links area. A small pen will appear, allowing you to click and edit this section.

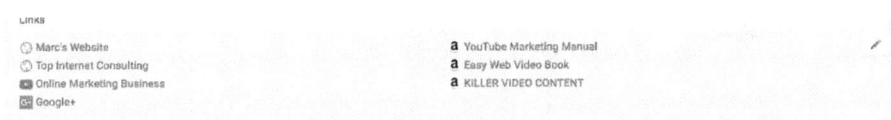

See the pen in the upper right corner?

Once the pen is clicked, you can add links.

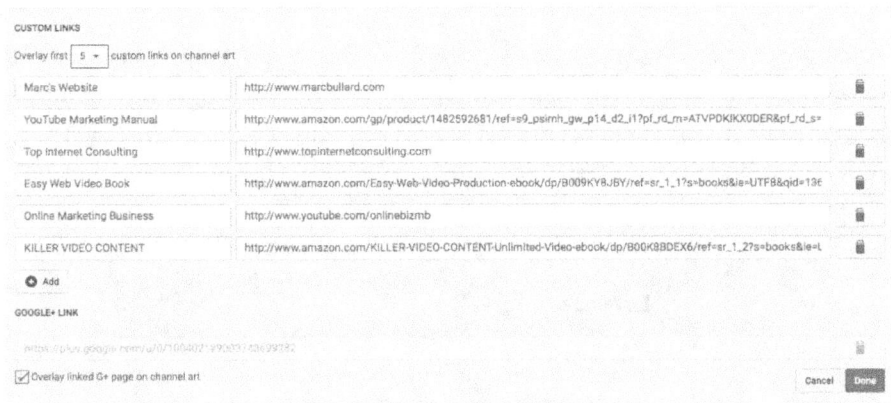

Add as many as you like but only up to 5 will be overlaid over the channel banner. And as always, make the first link your most important one (usually your website). Make sure you click 'Done' and then you have links added.

6. After the front end of your channel is set up, it's time to optimize the channel some more on the back end. To do this, you need to go to a special part of Youtube called the Video Manager. At the time of this writing, Youtube provides multiple ways to access the Video Manager. I will show you two methods, one of which is bound to work.
Make sure you're at your Youtube channel, you'll know you're there if you can see your banner.

When looking at your banner, you may see some links directly above providing information about subscribers and views along with a link to the video manager.

 1,353 subscribers   494,616 views   Video Manager

Video Manager is the third option.

Clicking Video Manager will take you there.

Optionally, some channels might not have the links above the banner. If that is the case, you might see two blue buttons underneath the banner, one to Edit Layout and the other for Creator Studio. Clicking 'Creator Studio' will bring you to the Video Manager (weird, I know).

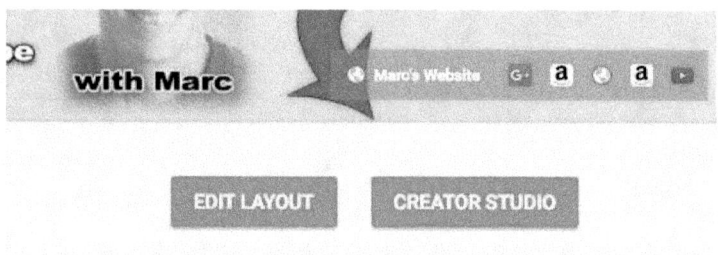

Click the Creator Studio button.

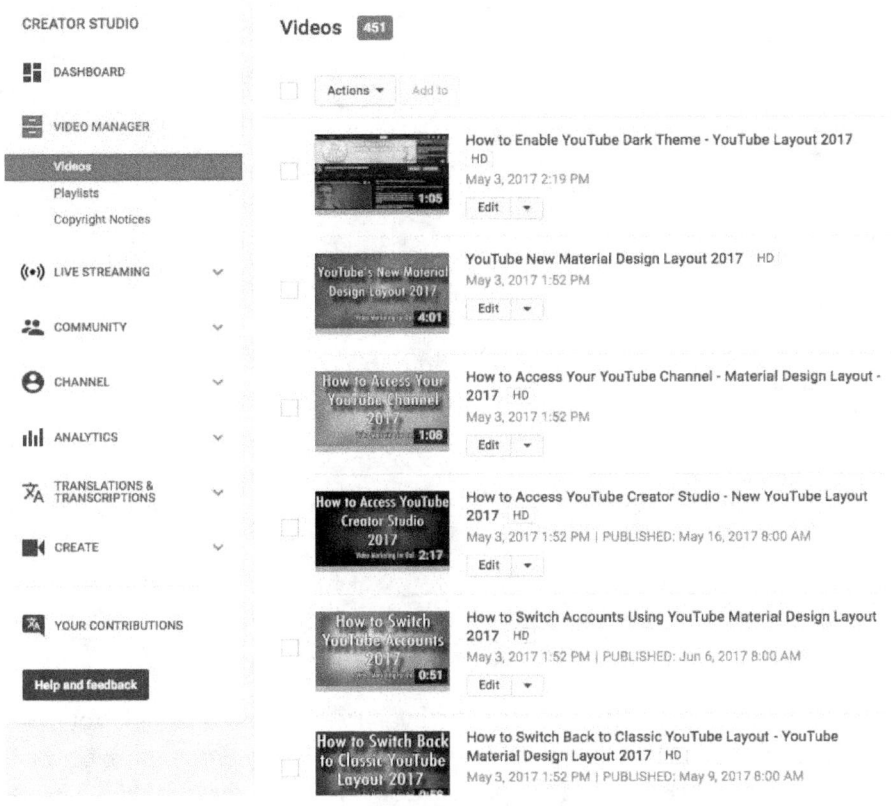

The menu on the left shows you are in the Video Manager.

The Video Manager is an area only available to you (when logged in) and shows all of your uploaded videos. Each video is listed in chronological order along the middle of the page. On the left is a new menu providing links to DASHBOARD, VIDEO MANAGER, LIVE STREAMING, COMMUNITY, CHANNEL, and others. We can further optimize your channel by clicking on the CHANNEL link from the left menu.

Once you click the CHANNEL link, you will be taken to a Status and Features page.

Status and Features page.

This page shows you what options are available for your channel. Your Youtube account is like a car with basic options. There are upgrades you can enable to really beef up the power. Some of these might not be eligible to you at first but don't worry, you'll get there. Don't worry too much about these options right now. The important thing here is to click another link on the left menu. Located under CHANNEL, you will see an option for Advanced. Click that.

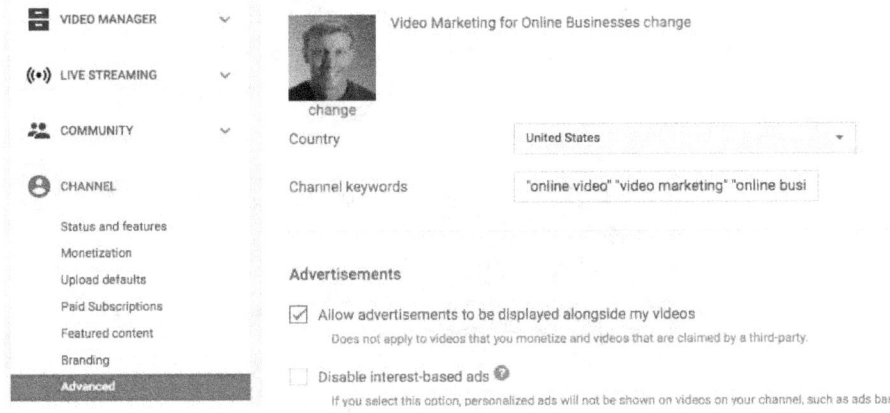

Advanced Account Page.

You are now at the Account page. Here you will see information about your Youtube account such as the name of your account, Country, and Channel Keywords. Channel Keywords is the area you need to be aware of. Here you can enter words or phrases that are related to your business (remember the list I provided earlier). I suggest putting in anywhere from 6-12 keywords and/or keyword phrases in this area. These keywords will help in the Youtube search results as well as Google's. Definitely put something in here. Again, these aren't set in stone so you can add some now and add/remove some later, if needed. Once you add some keywords, be sure to click the blue 'Save' button at the bottom of the page. There are other advanced options on this page. Don't worry about those for now. The Channel Keywords are the absolute most important thing on this page.

7. The next thing you want to do is make sure that every one of your videos are optimized for the search engines. **Optimizing your video information is going to make the difference between getting found on YouTube/Google or not. There's many ways to optimize your videos, but the three most powerful are optimizing your title, description, and tags.** To do this, go back to your Video Manager. If you're still on the Account page,

simply clicking the 'Video Manager' link in the left menu will take you there. Once you're there, click the small 'Edit' button next to the thumbnail of any of your videos.

Click the small 'Edit' button.

You will now be on the 'Info and Settings' page. This is where you can edit your video information.

YouTube New Material Design Layout 2017

Info and Settings Page.

Title

The title is extremely important. It's one of the first things Youtube and viewers see in Youtube's search results. It also shows up in Google results. Putting keywords in your Youtube title is the first of many things you should do to your uploaded videos. Keywords are words or phrases that the average web surfer would type into a search box in order to get more information on whatever subject they are interested in. Every business has certain keywords related to them, for example: An online health food store would want to get people looking for 'organic', 'vegan', or 'omega-3' as these are words that are being typed into the search bar by a health food store's potential customer.

Now let's say there were two online health food stores. Store 1 makes a video that talks about all of the benefits of some new vitamins. When it comes time to enter in the title, they put 'Check out these new vitamins'. Store 2 also makes a video about the same vitamins but they put in the title 'Vegan Vitamins - Daily Dose of Omega-3s'.

The second store's video will be seen by a lot more people. Not only that, the people going to see Store 2's video are going to be a more targeted niche, particularly those who are interested in either 'vegan' things, 'omega-3s' or both. You can now cater to that niche more exclusively.

I do have a word of warning about the above example. When you title your videos, they must be related to what the video is about. If Store 2 had used that title but the vitamins didn't have any of those benefits, people will click away, possibly losing a potential customer or sale. Nobody likes to be tricked. Be sure to be truthful in your titles. Not only that, Youtube lets viewers 'Report' videos. To 'Report' a video means that Youtube now knows your video didn't sit right with that viewer for whatever reason. If the video gets 'Reported' too much, Youtube may take down that video or even disable your account.

The dreaded 'Report'

Just so you know, be sure to put the most valuable keywords closest to the beginning of the title. For example, if your video is about YouTube Marketing, you want to try to put the phrase 'YouTube Marketing' near the beginning. The title would have more search engine value if you title it 'YouTube Marketing – Put Keywords in your title' compared to 'Want to Learn YouTube Marketing?'

YouTube Marketing Tips - YouTube New Material Design Layout 2017

Description

The next box you encounter is the Description box. The description box is a great place to enter text on what your video is about. Youtube looks at what you put in the description box, so it's good to put keywords in your description.

Now don't go typing in a list of keywords in your description box, you have to sprinkle them into your description and they have to sound natural. Take a look at a correctly formatted description below.

Video Marketing for Online Businesses
Published on May 23, 2017

http://www.marcbullard.com How to Turn On and Turn Off Restricted Mode - YouTube Material Design Layout 2017
This mode provides you with different buttons than the older YouTube layouts. You can enable these options, watch the video to see how.

Marc is Head Instructor at the Internet Marketing Training Center of Virginia - http://www.imtcva.org

Marc's Marketing Course - 60% OFF NO FLUFF VIDEO MARKETING: https://www.udemy.com/no-fluff-youtub...

Marc's Book YOUTUBE MARKETING MANUAL: http://www.amazon.com/dp/B00BJP4XYO

Marc's Book KILLER VIDEO CONTENT: http://amzn.to/1k5Ut6b

Subscribe: http://www.youtube.com/user/videoMTC

How to Use YouTube Live Events for Your Business: https://www.udemy.com/how-to-use-yout...

What's all this about? Video marketing, specifically YouTube marketing has quickly turned into one of the most powerful Internet marketing tools available. With little more than a camera and a microphone, anybody can use the power of the Internet to be seen and heard.

If you're an author, consultant, small business owner, or anybody that wants publicity online, you need to understand video marketing. Discover YouTube's secrets, implement a marketing plan, and showcase your brand like never before. It's all here. You'll find a detailed breakdown of keyword strategies, optimizing techniques for videos and channels, marketing tactics, advertising opportunities, and crucial metrics & analysis tools.

Description Box.

The first thing you see is some HTML code, more specifically, a website URL. We'll get to that in a moment. Take a look at the paragraph after the code. It gives information on the same subject as the video title above. Also, there are keywords such as 'youtube layout', 'youtube material design', and 'restricted mode'. This is how you should have every one of your descriptions, with your own keywords of course. But what about that HTML code at the beginning?

The HTML code, that stuff starting with 'http://.....', is the actual website link to wherever you want your viewers to click to. This can be your blog, website, landing page, sales page, or anywhere else that you want to send your potential customers. The way it is typed out is the only way Youtube will allow a click-able link in your description box.

So why do you need to put a link to your site in the description box anyway? People watching your video may like the information you are giving them and are now interested in getting more information or purchasing your products. Putting a click-able link right there in the description box is the easiest way for them to get to your site. Sure, they could type it out, but I promise you there are people out there that are too lazy to do it. I know I'm like that sometimes. So let's make it easy for them.

Now, why did I put the URL to my site as the first thing in the description box? For a couple of reasons. Let's look at a typical Youtube page:

How to Turn On and Turn Off Restricted Mode - YouTube Material Design Layout 2017
2,594 views   13   7

Video Marketing for Online Businesses
Published on May 23, 2017

http://www.marcbullard.com How to Turn On and Turn Off Restricted Mode - YouTube Material Design Layout 2017
This mode provides you with different buttons than the older YouTube layouts. You can enable
SHOW MORE

Description only shows a few lines.

Here we see what a typical viewer gets to when he searches for and clicks on a video. In the photo above, you see the title of the video, and the username of the uploader. There are also a 'play/pause' button for the video and other controls. Underneath all of that you see the beginning of our description. The description is cut off but there is a button that allows you to 'Show more'. If you click on the 'Show more' button, the rest of the description can be seen.

Once the 'Show more' button is clicked, viewers can see the rest of the description. The problem for you is that most people don't bother clicking the 'Show more' button. That means if you put your click-able link anywhere but the top of the description box, a lot of people won't see it. That's one reason why you want to put it in the beginning. The other reason to put it there is because it is located right in the line of vision to our viewer. If the viewer needs to pause, play, adjust the volume, or any number of things in the area of the video player, the link to your site is in the same general area.

Why is this link so important? Since the description box is the only place on the video watch page Youtube allows you to put a click-able link, that also means it's the only place anywhere on the page that a viewer can click to your site. It's very valuable.

Tags Box

The 'Tags' box is the third most important place to optimize your video. This is another place you should put relevant keywords. It's important to fill out the 'Tags' box with keyword terms that are related to the video. You can use up to 120 characters in the tags box. A good rule of thumb is to have no more than 6-20 tags in the tags box, so pick the best, most relevant tags you can. In order to provide its users with the best results, Youtube pays a lot of attention to tags, and that's why you should too.

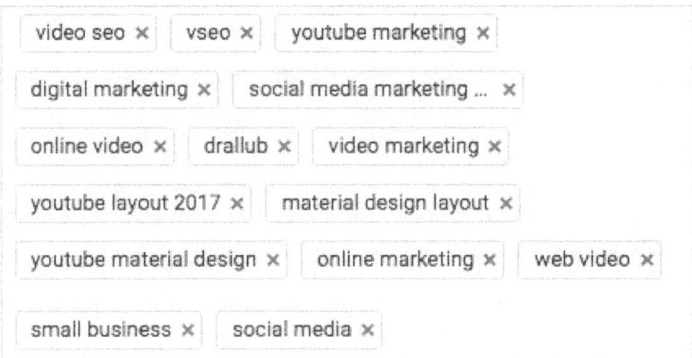

Tags Area.

Optimization of your Title, Description, and Tags is the 2nd most important thing you can do for your Youtube marketing efforts. What is the number 1 most important thing you should do in order to get the full marketing power of Youtube? Simple, it's to create more content. As basic as that sounds, it's where most people fail, but they don't have to.

This is just the basic starter kit for your Youtube channel. There are more, and just as important, Youtube marketing techniques you can (and should) use. Would you like to know how to:

- Find your competition's keywords
- Develop a content strategy proven to work
- Use your competitor's videos to grow your online visibility - piggyback off of their videos
- Analyze your videos to discover new traffic sources
- Boost popularity of your videos with comments
- Link and promote your videos with advanced strategies
- Create more content for your channel and never run out of ideas
- Brand your business even before somebody clicks to watch one of your videos

- Create evergreen videos that build your online presence 24/7
- Make uploading and optimizing easy as can be
- Connect your channel with your website to build trust with Youtube
- Much more

I can help you with all of these and provide results. I'm open to teaching you and your staff what they need to do and/or I can do it for you myself. Additionally, I offer videography services as well. I can shoot, edit, and upload optimized videos to your very own Youtube channel, increasing exposure and selling more homes. Let's get started!

Thanks for your time.

Marc Bullard
bullard.marc@gmail.com
MarcBullard.com

www.ingramcontent.com/pod-product-compliance
Lightning Source LLC
Chambersburg PA
CBHW071223240526
45470CB00018B/2297